# Beautiful Patterns
# And At Home Designs
# Coloring Book For Adults

## By Peaceful Mind Adult Coloring Books

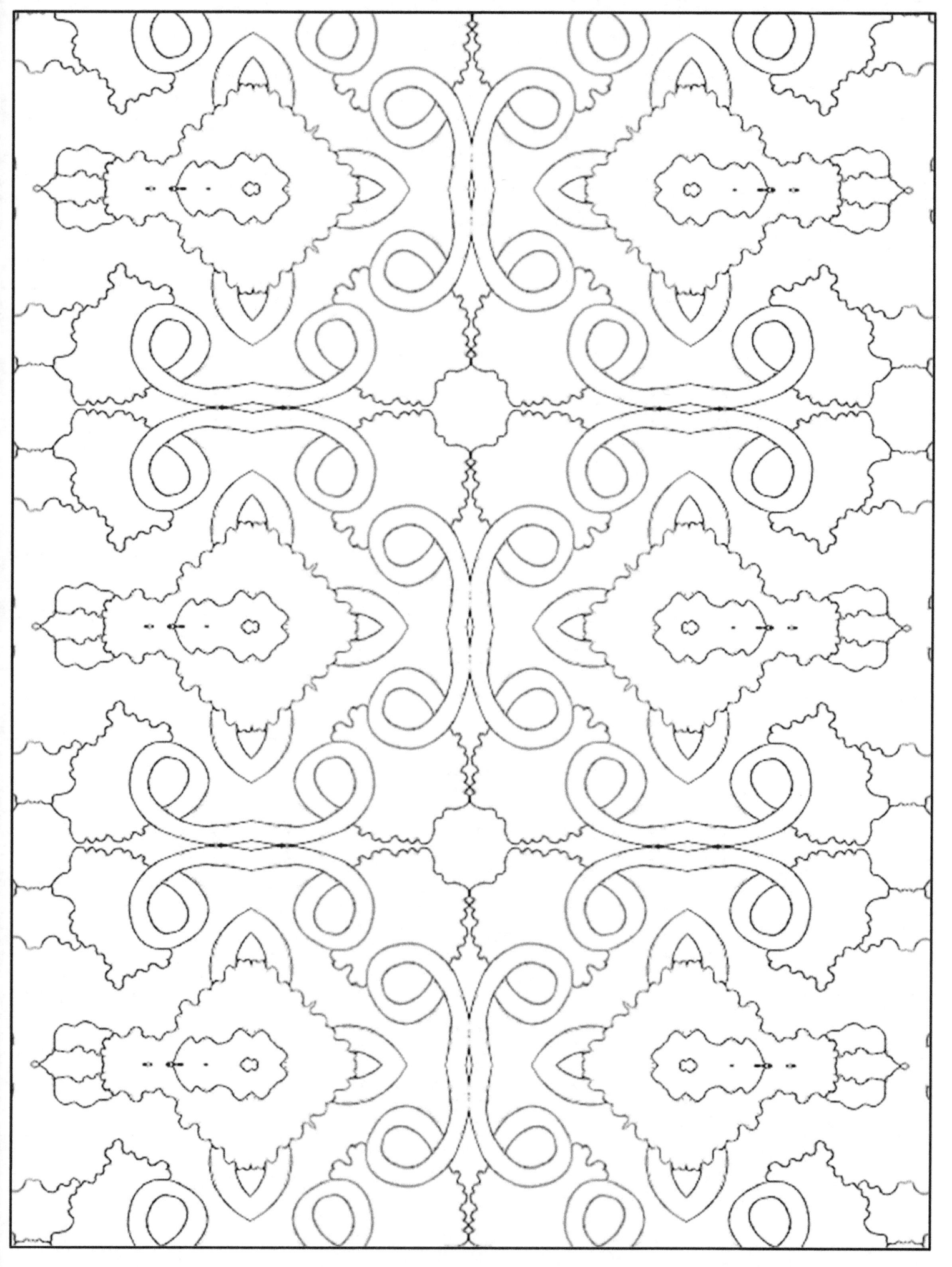

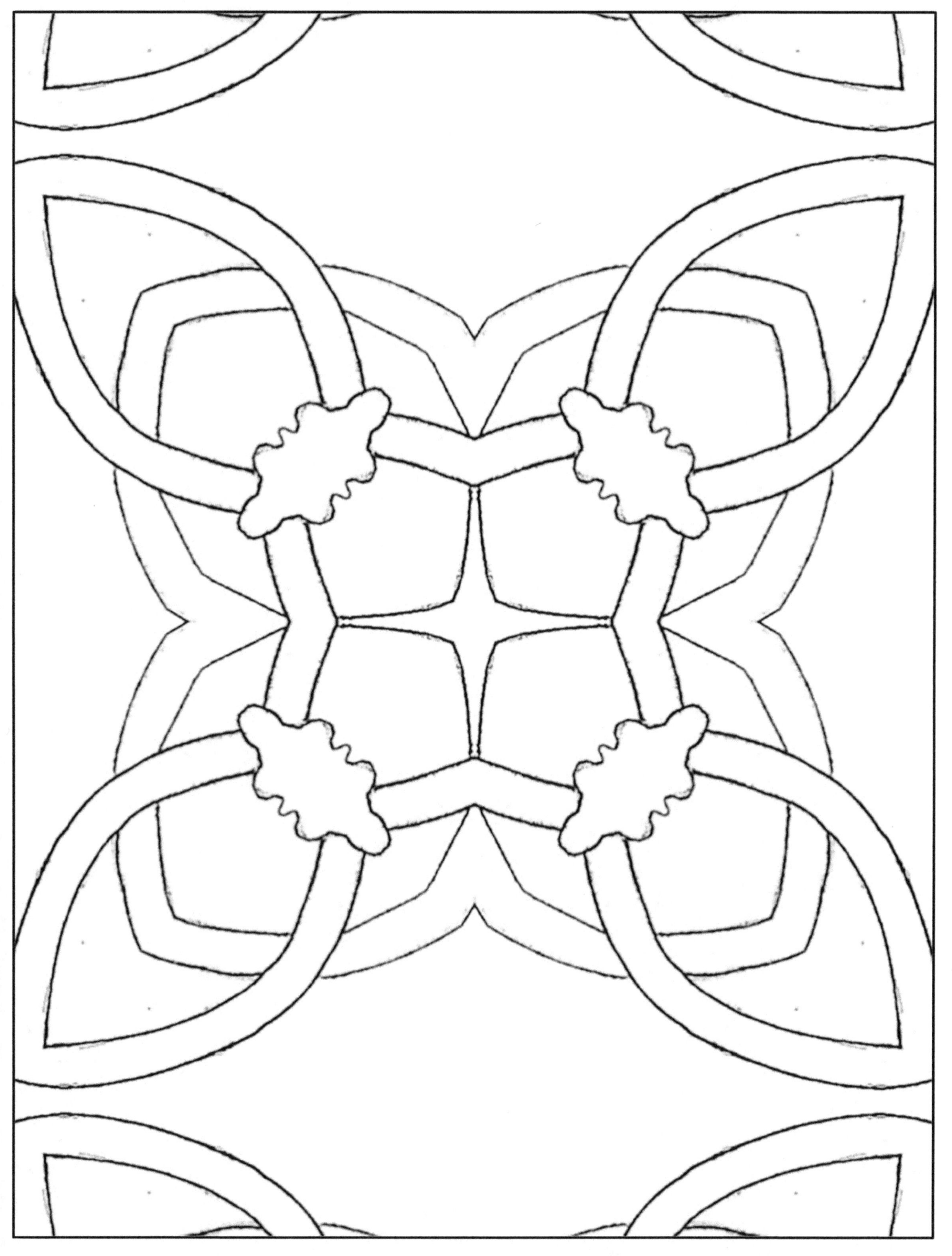

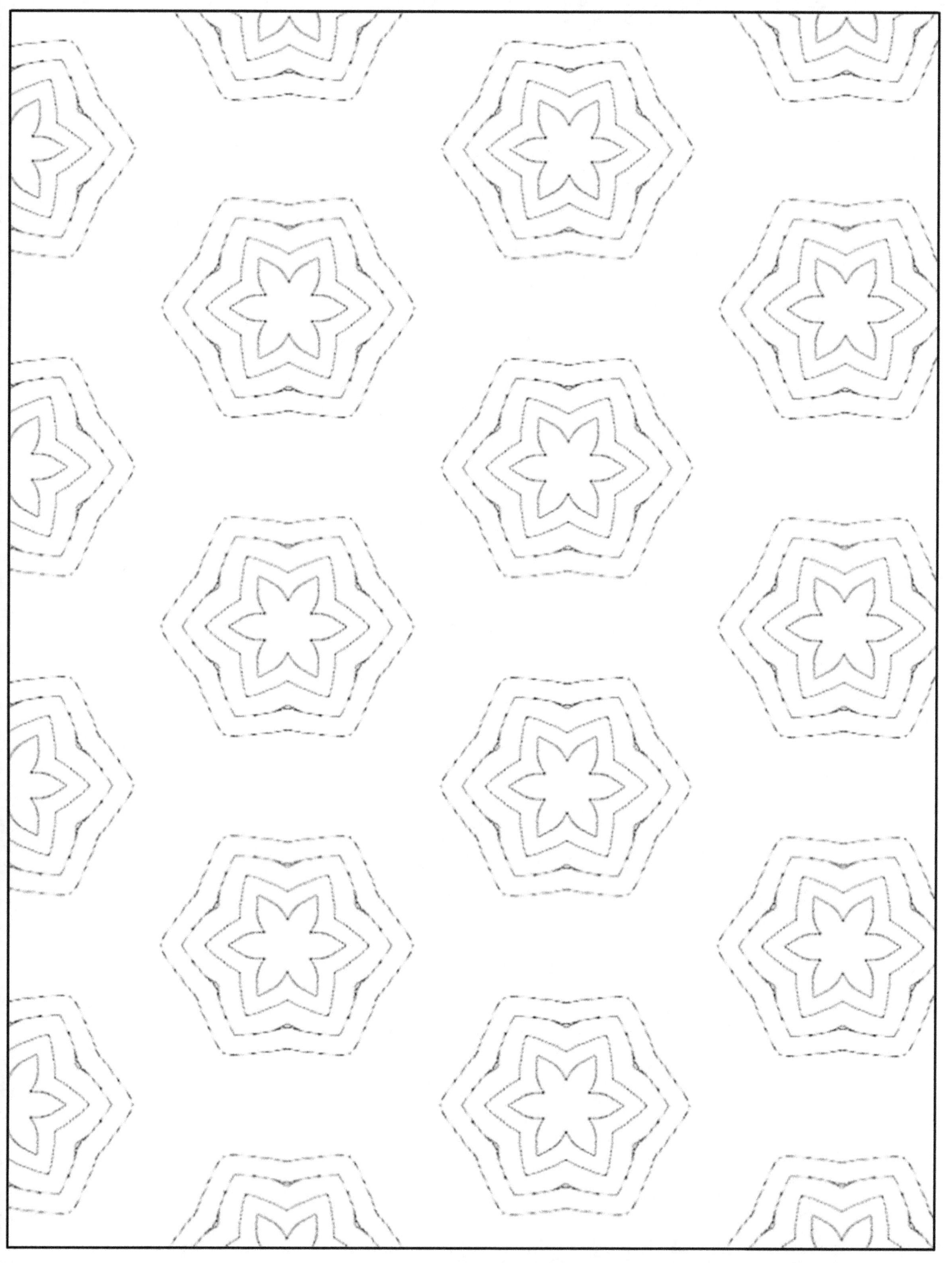

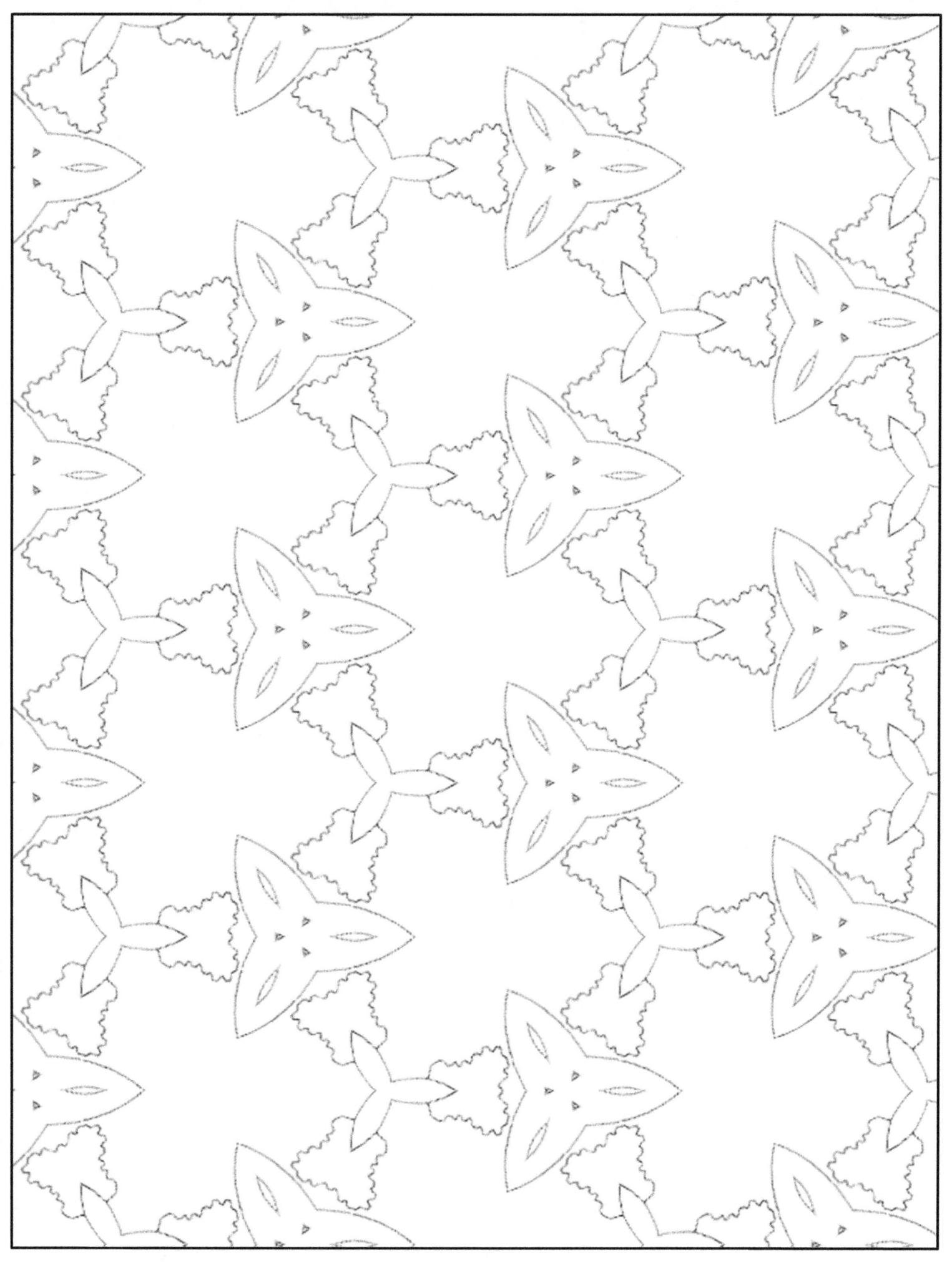

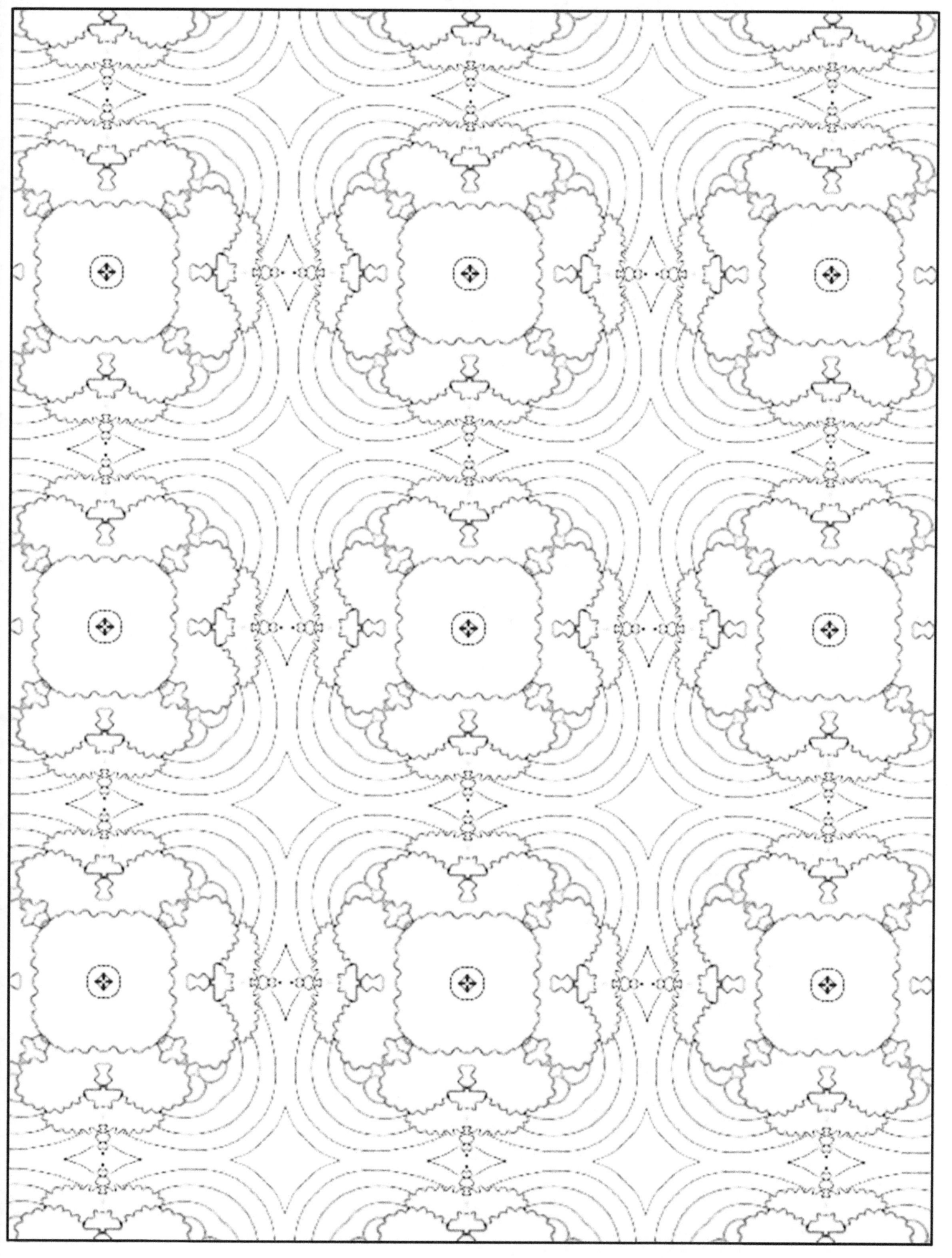

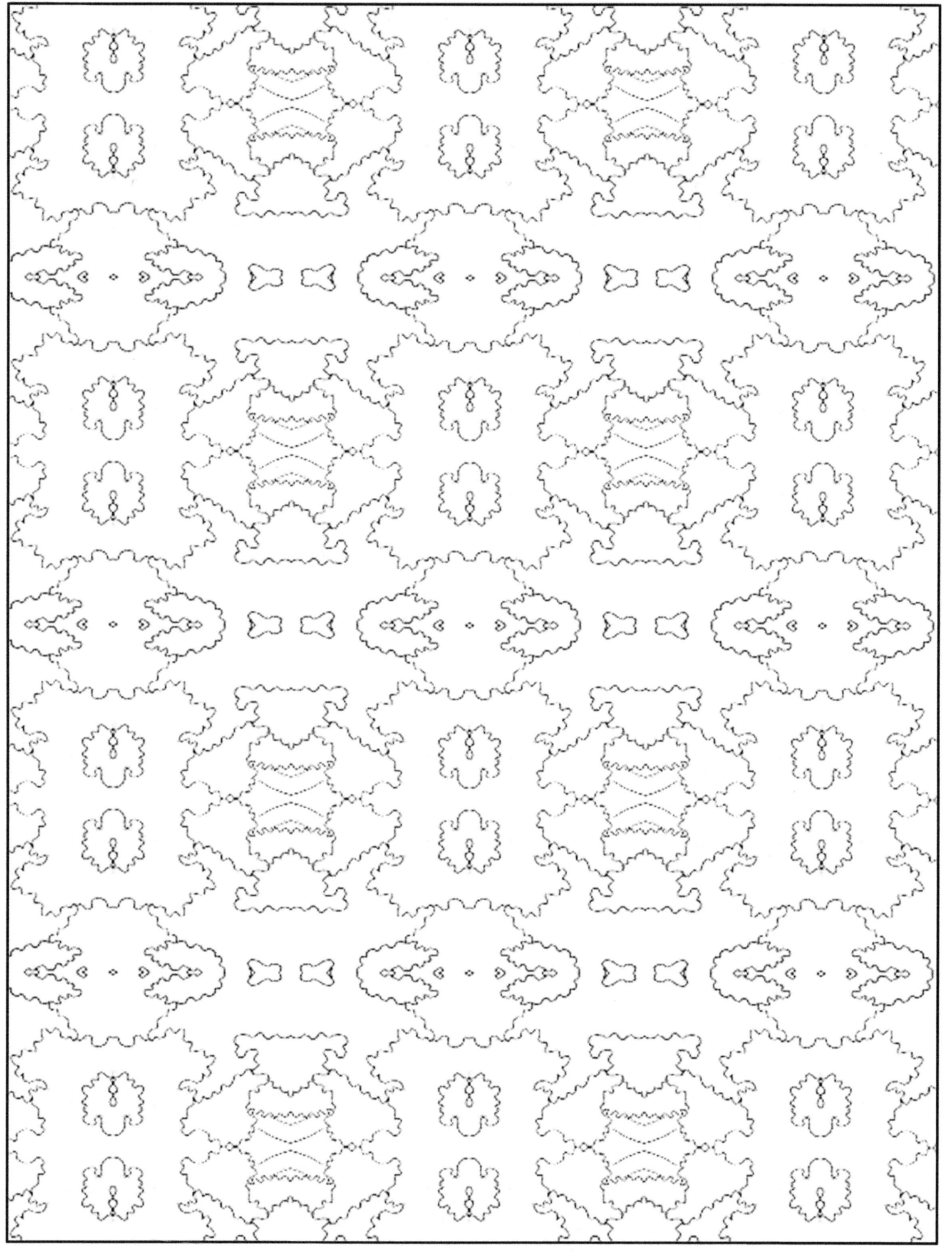

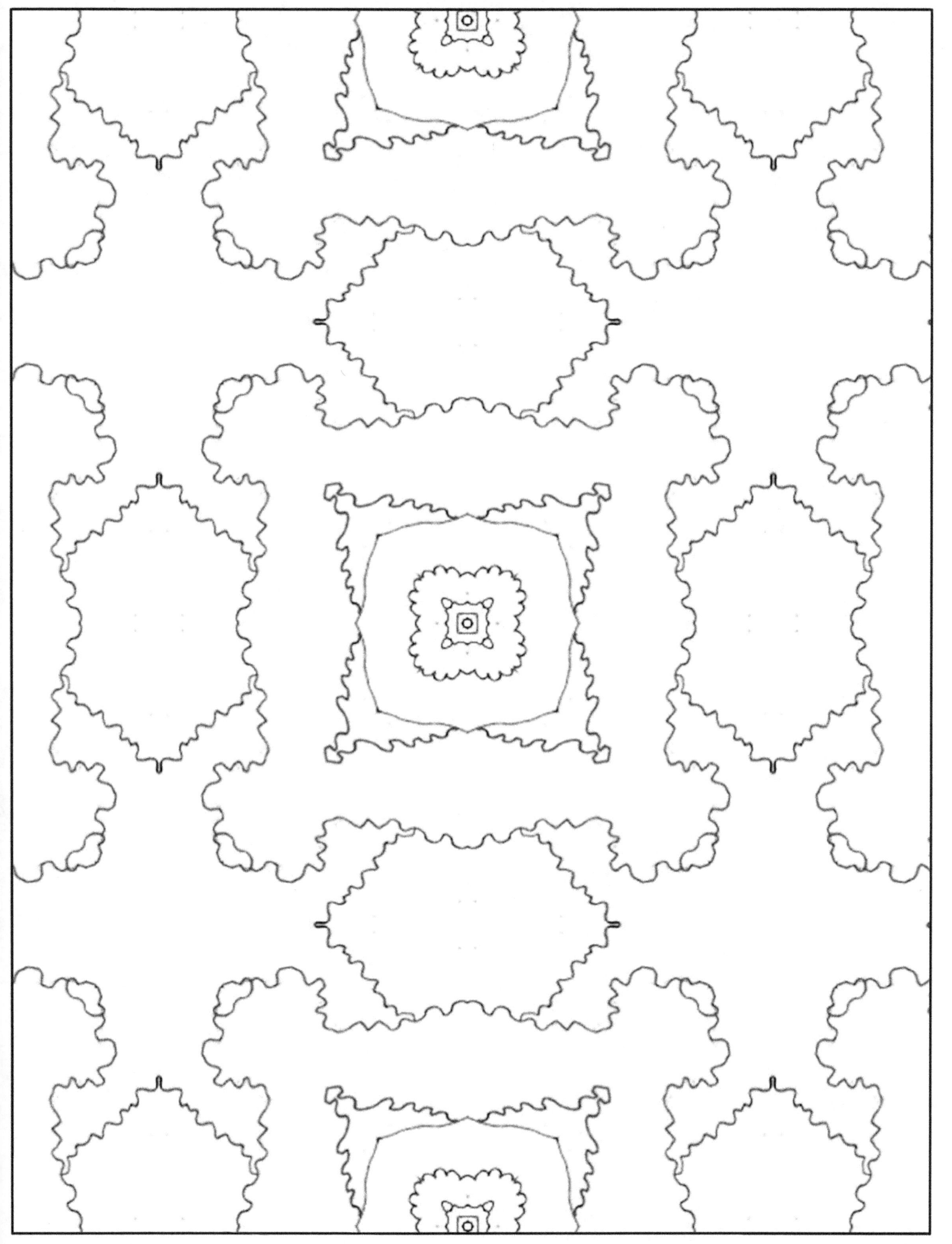

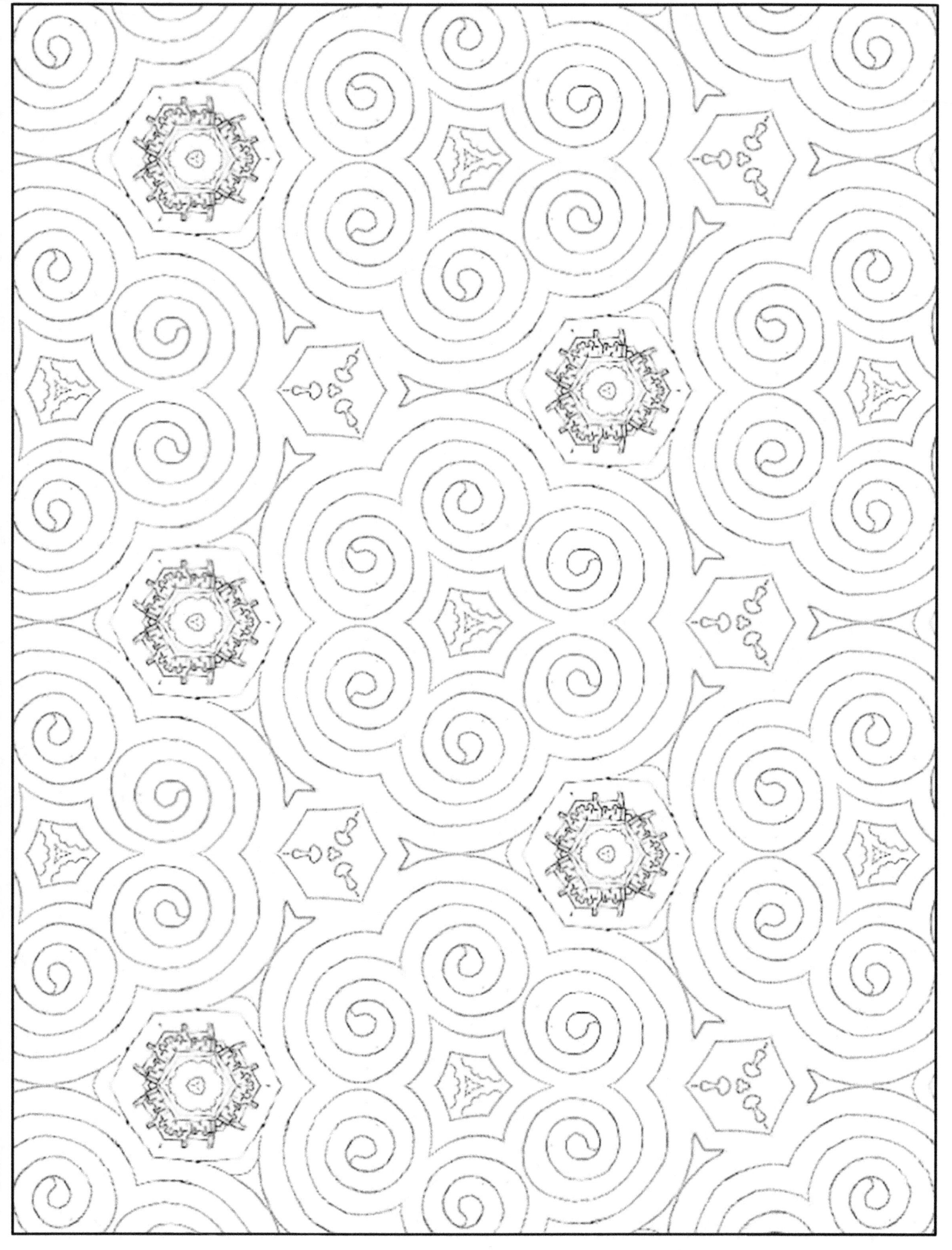

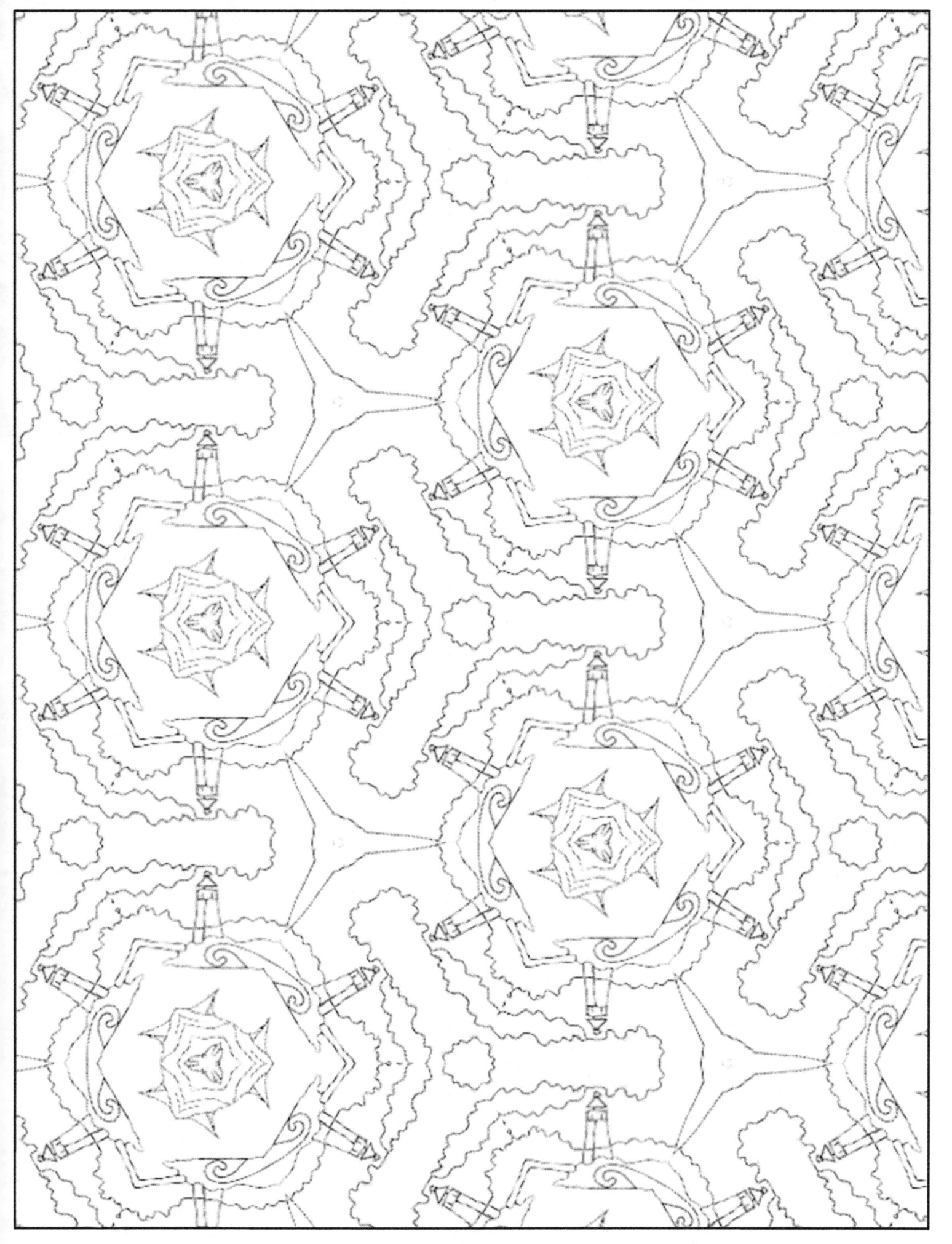

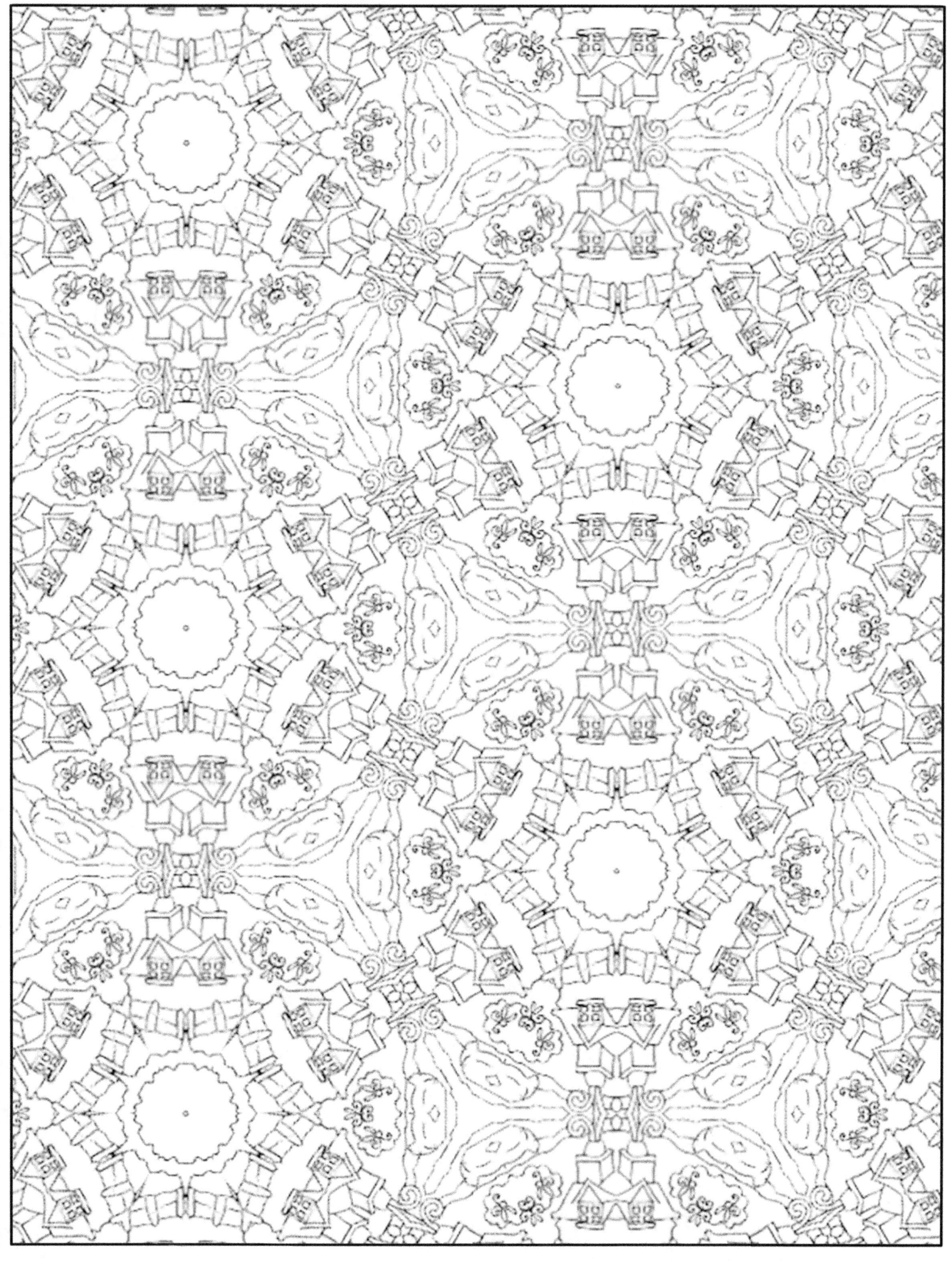

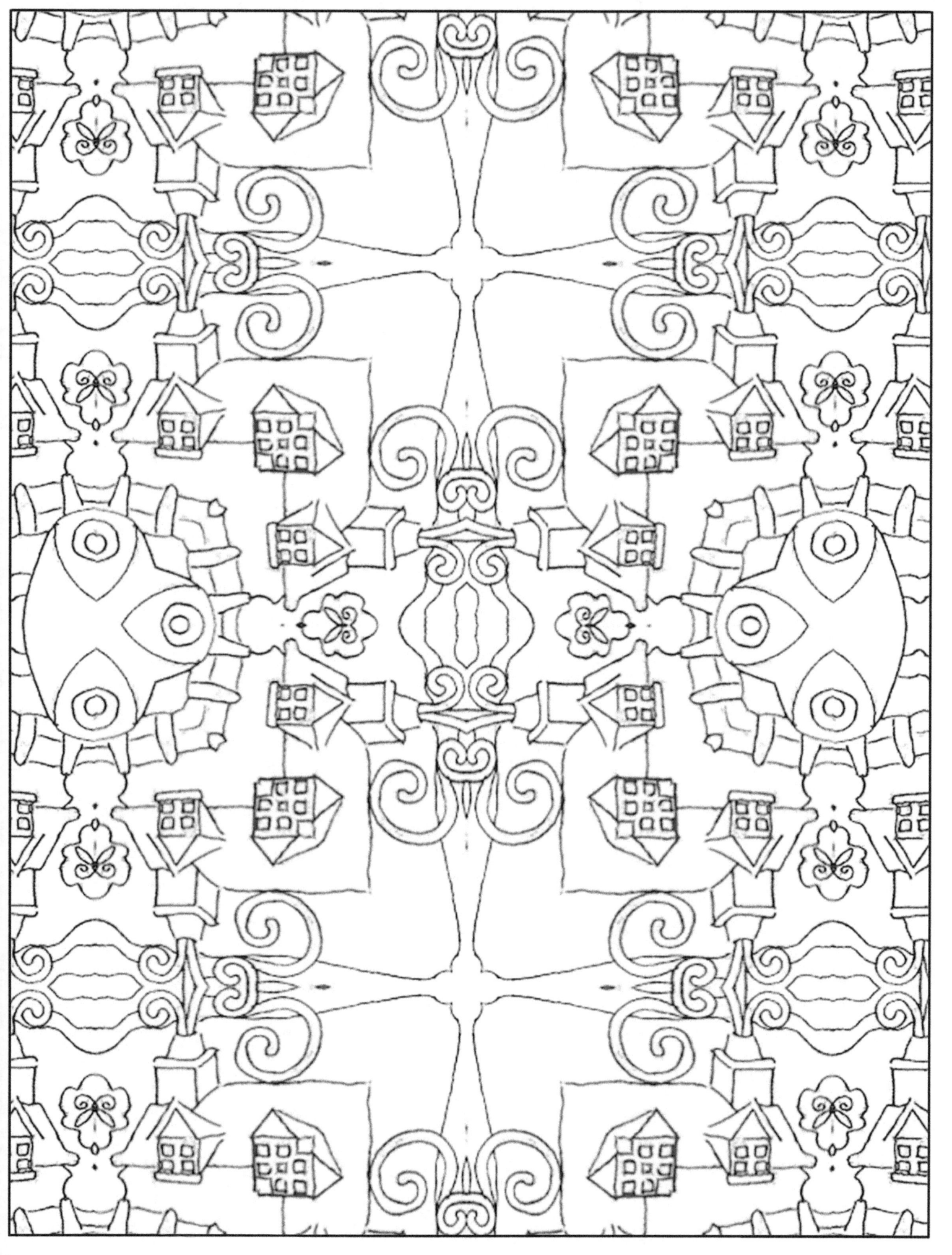

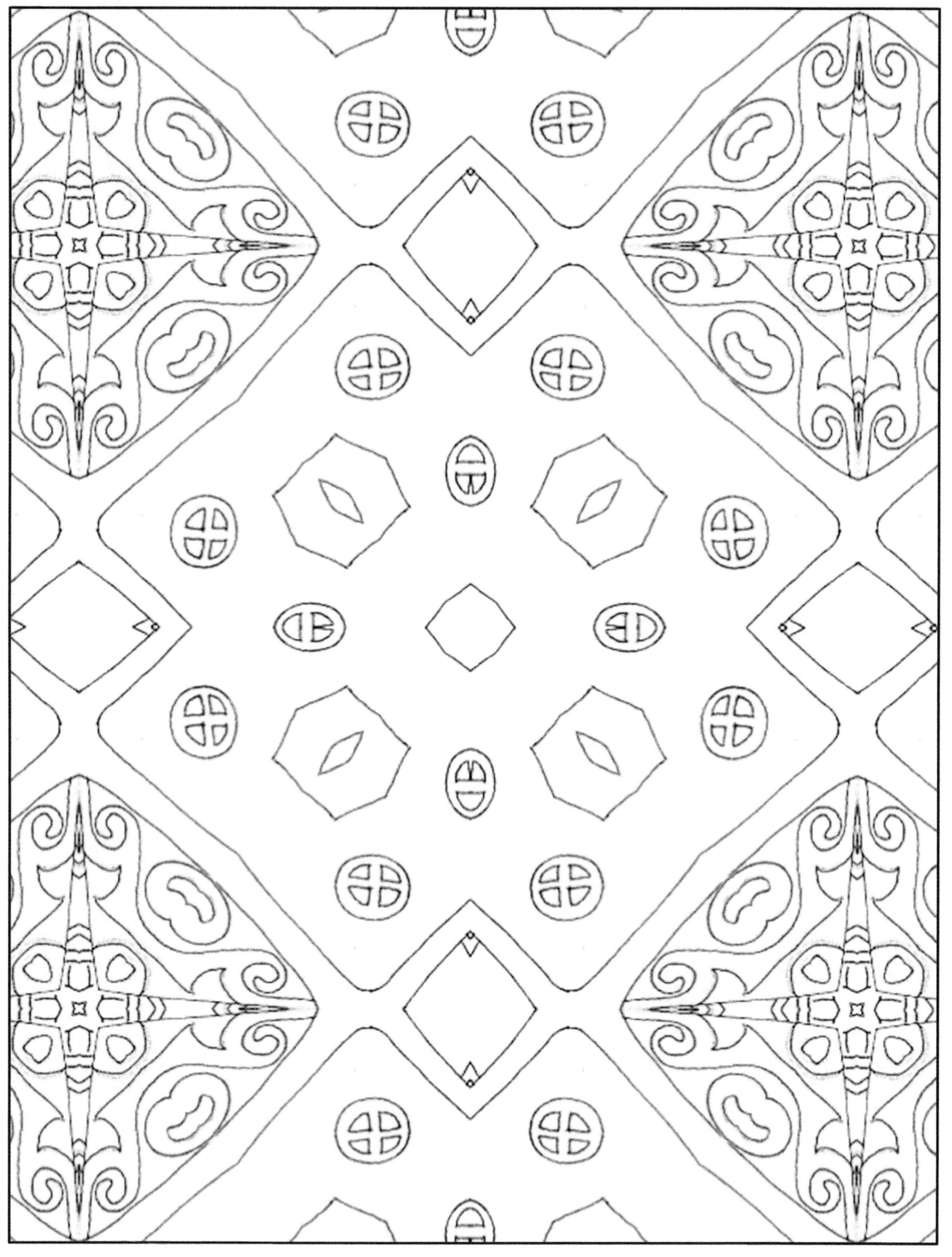

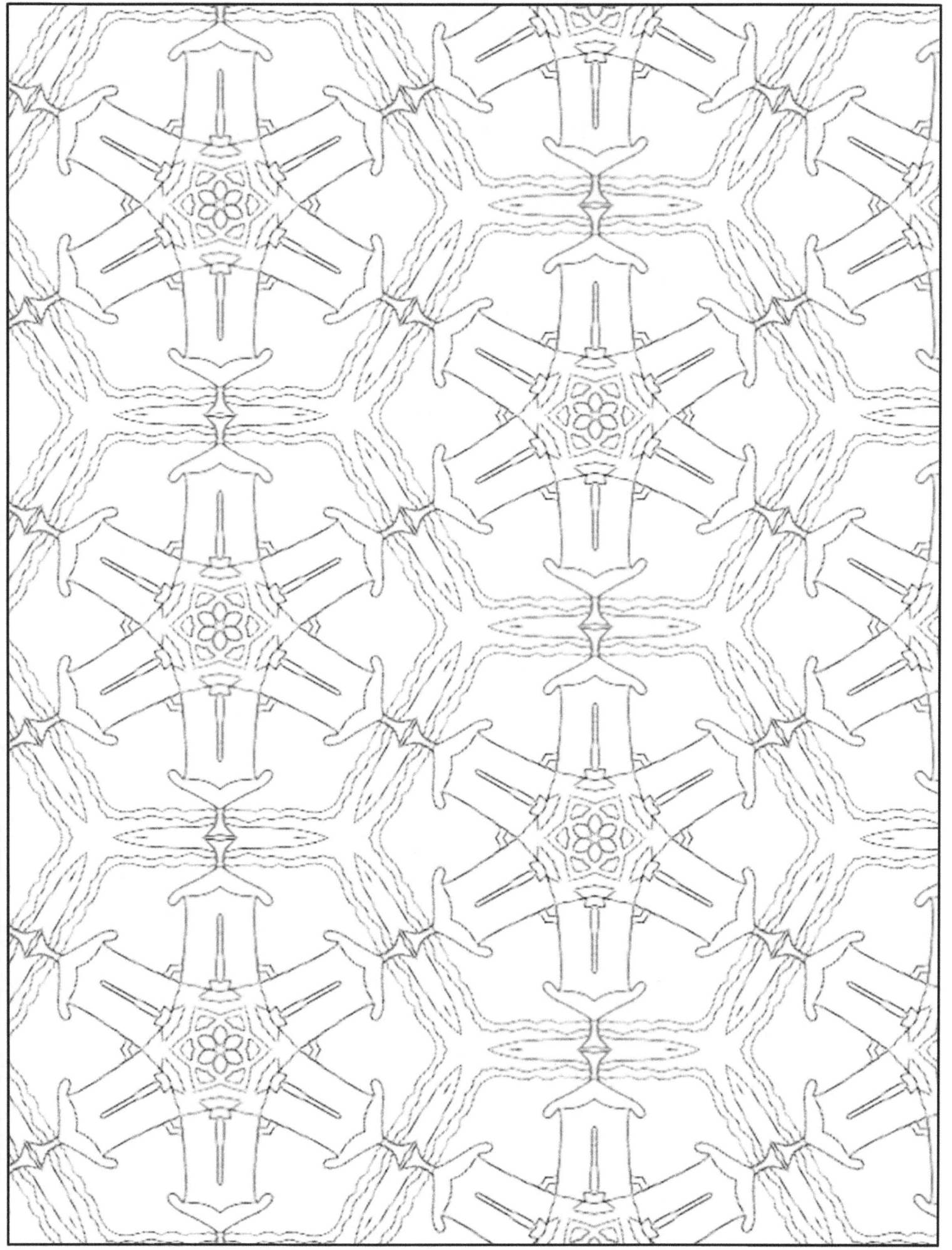

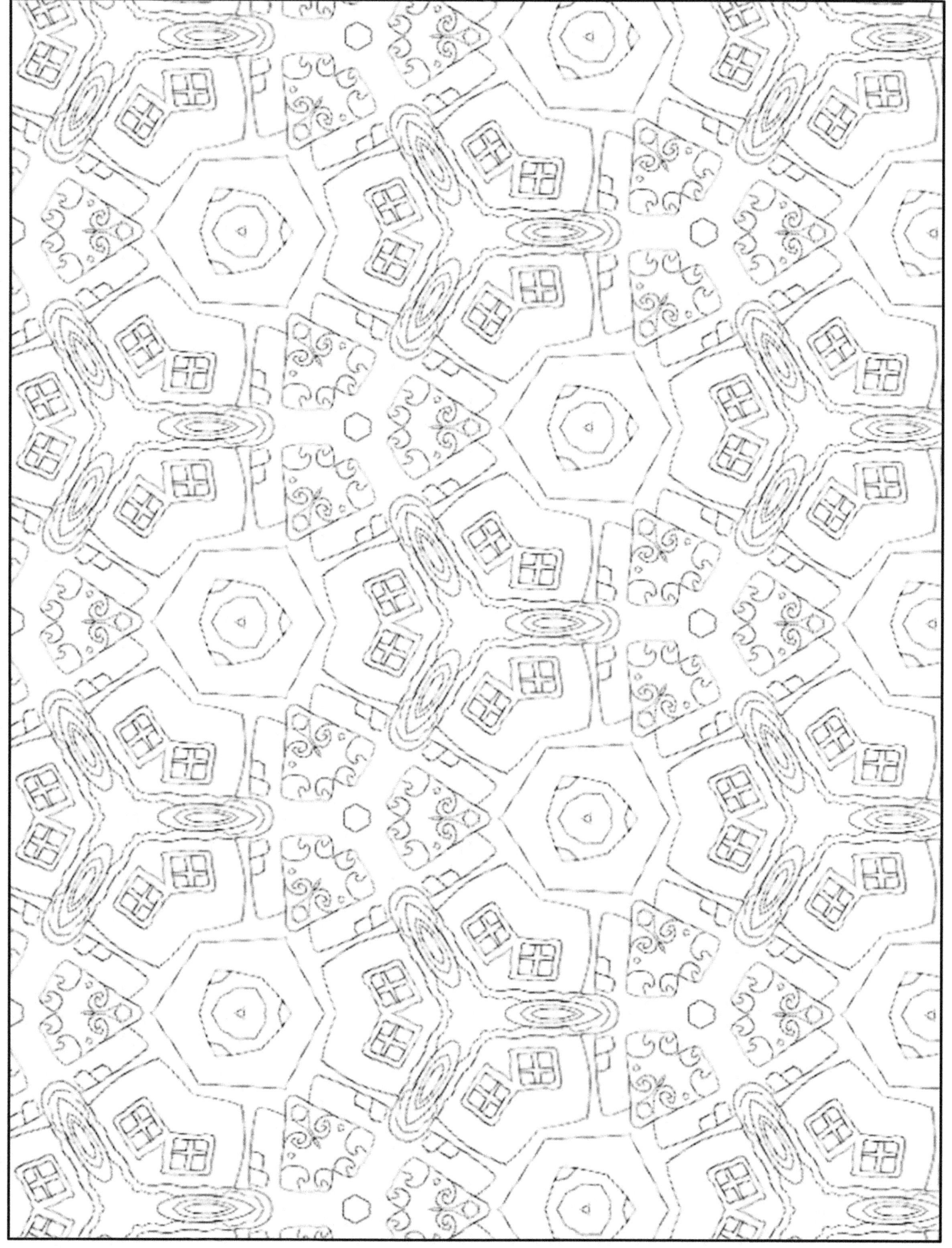

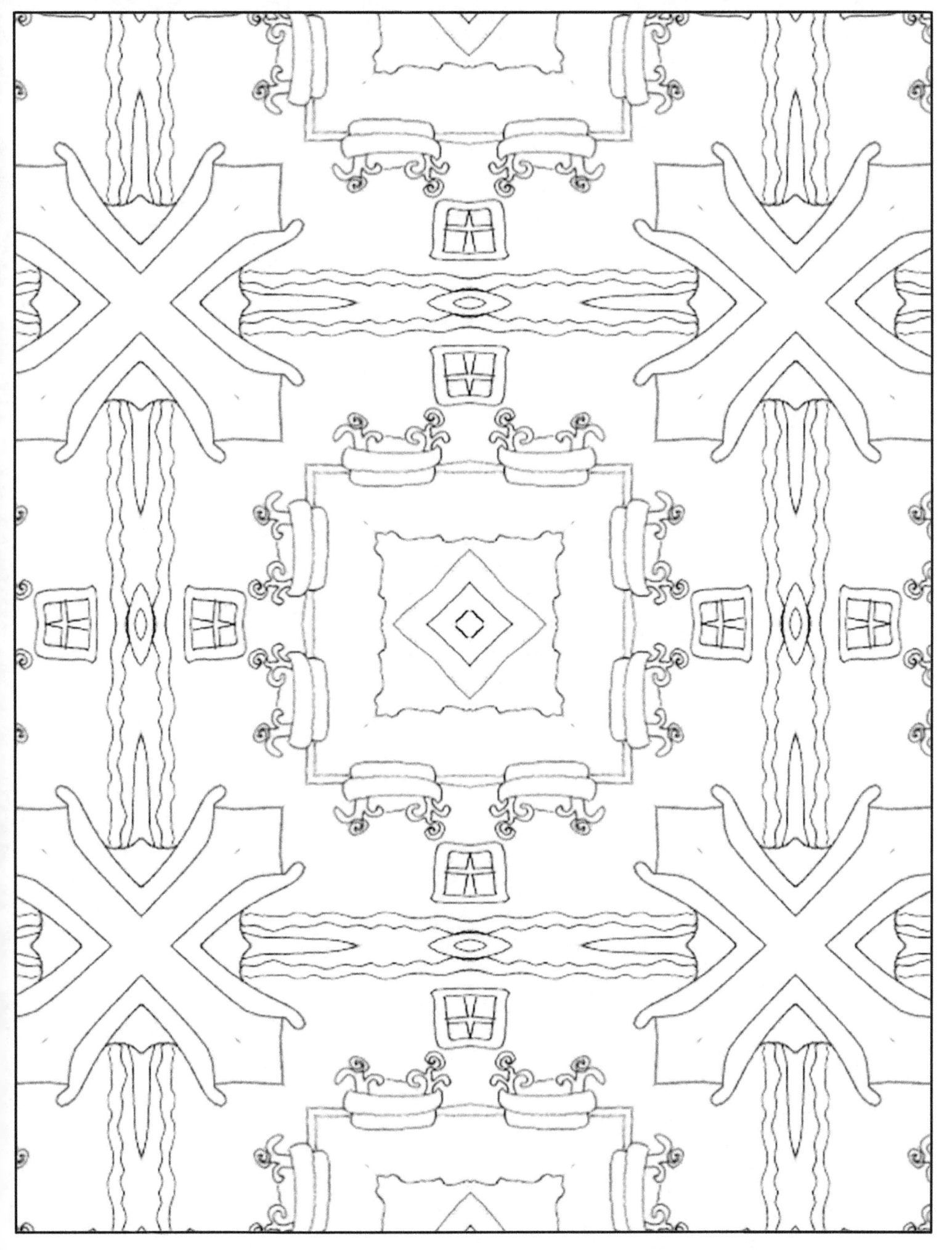

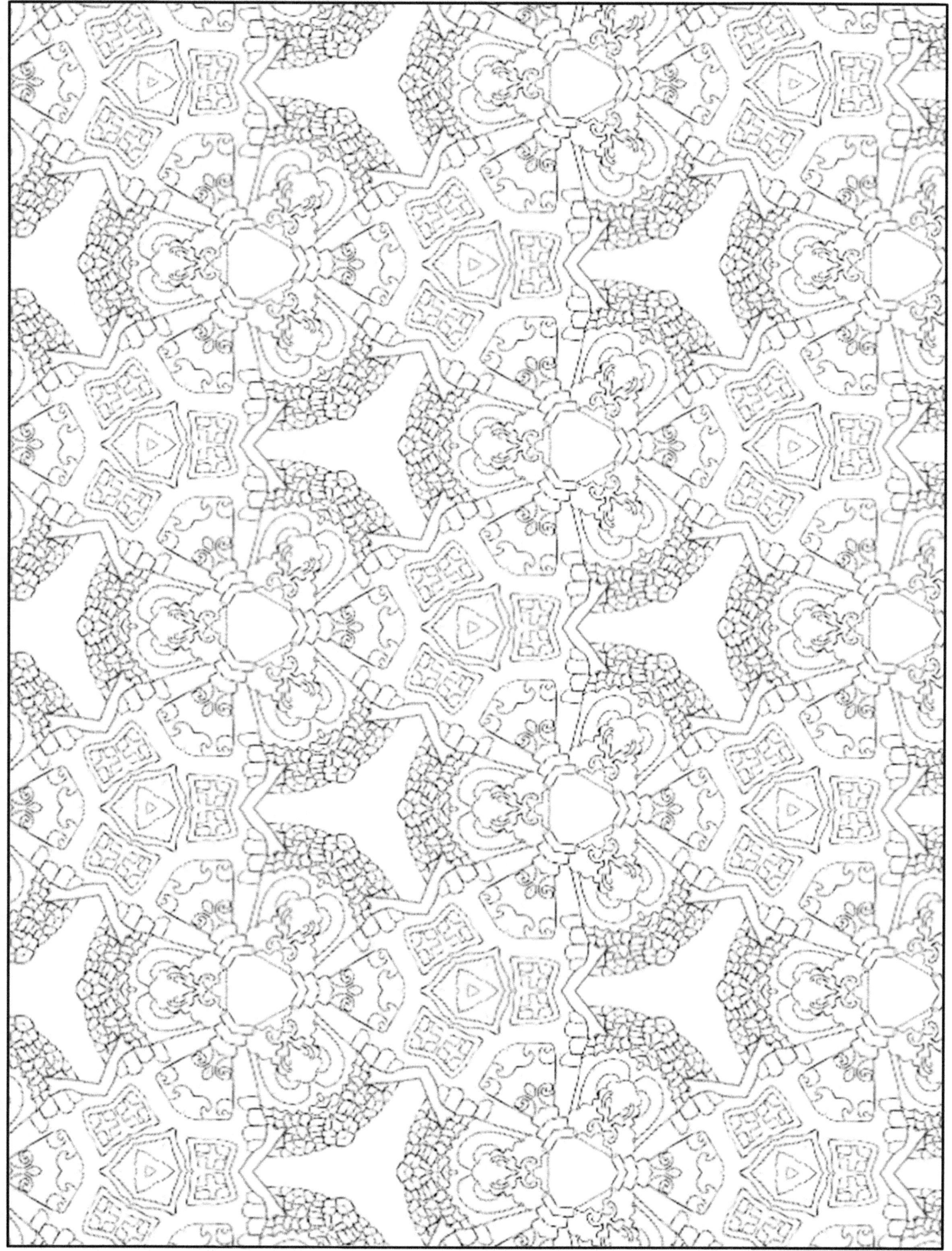

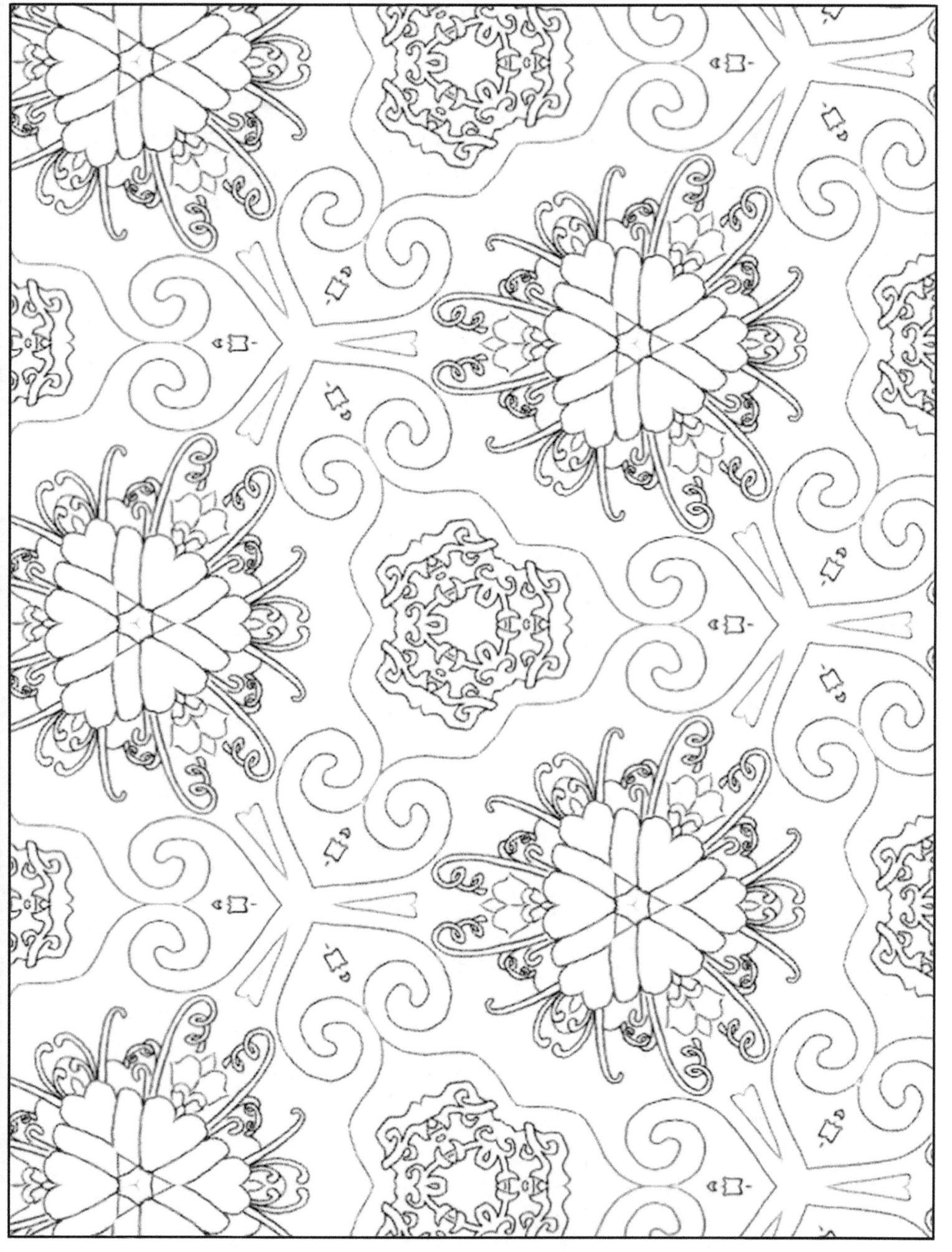

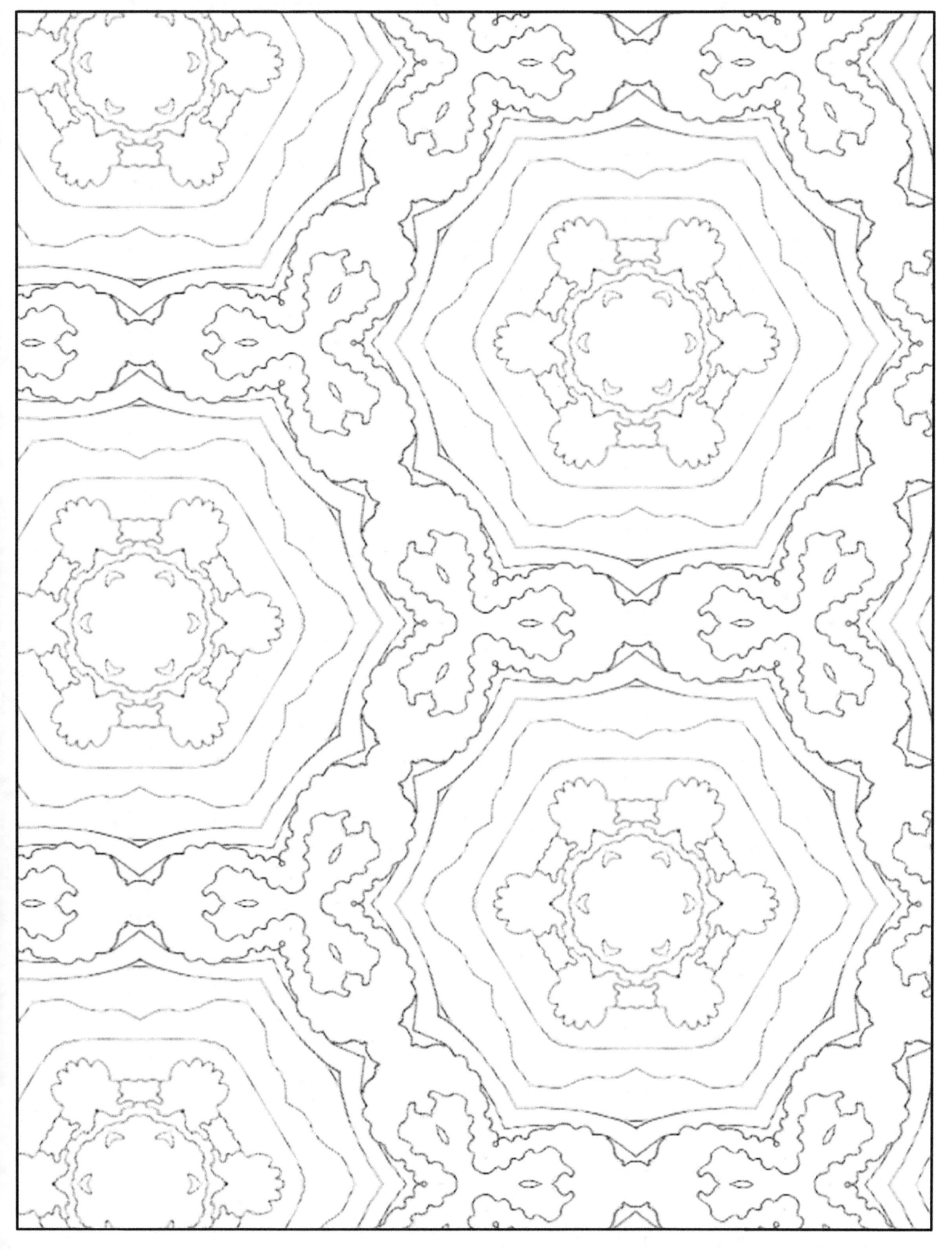

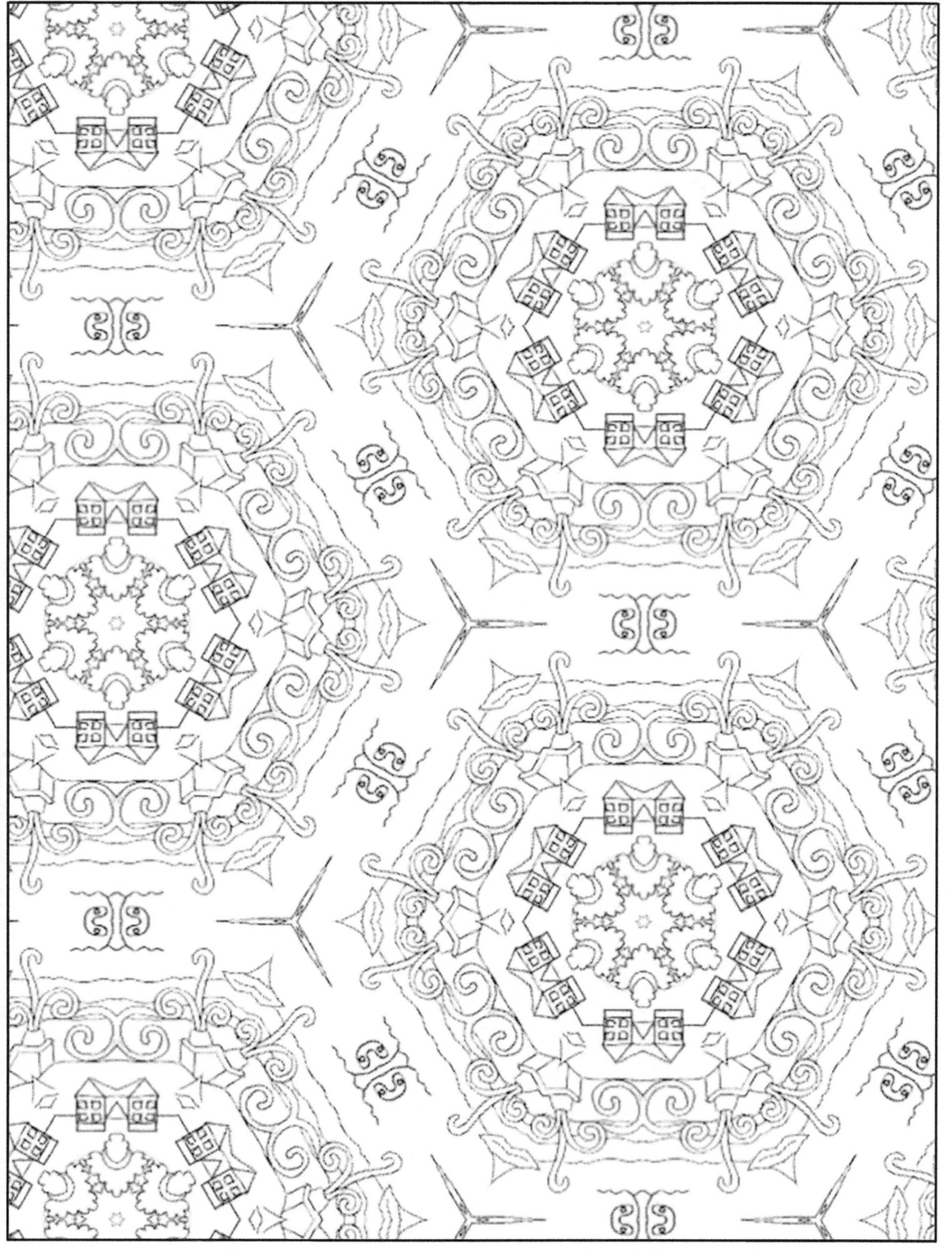

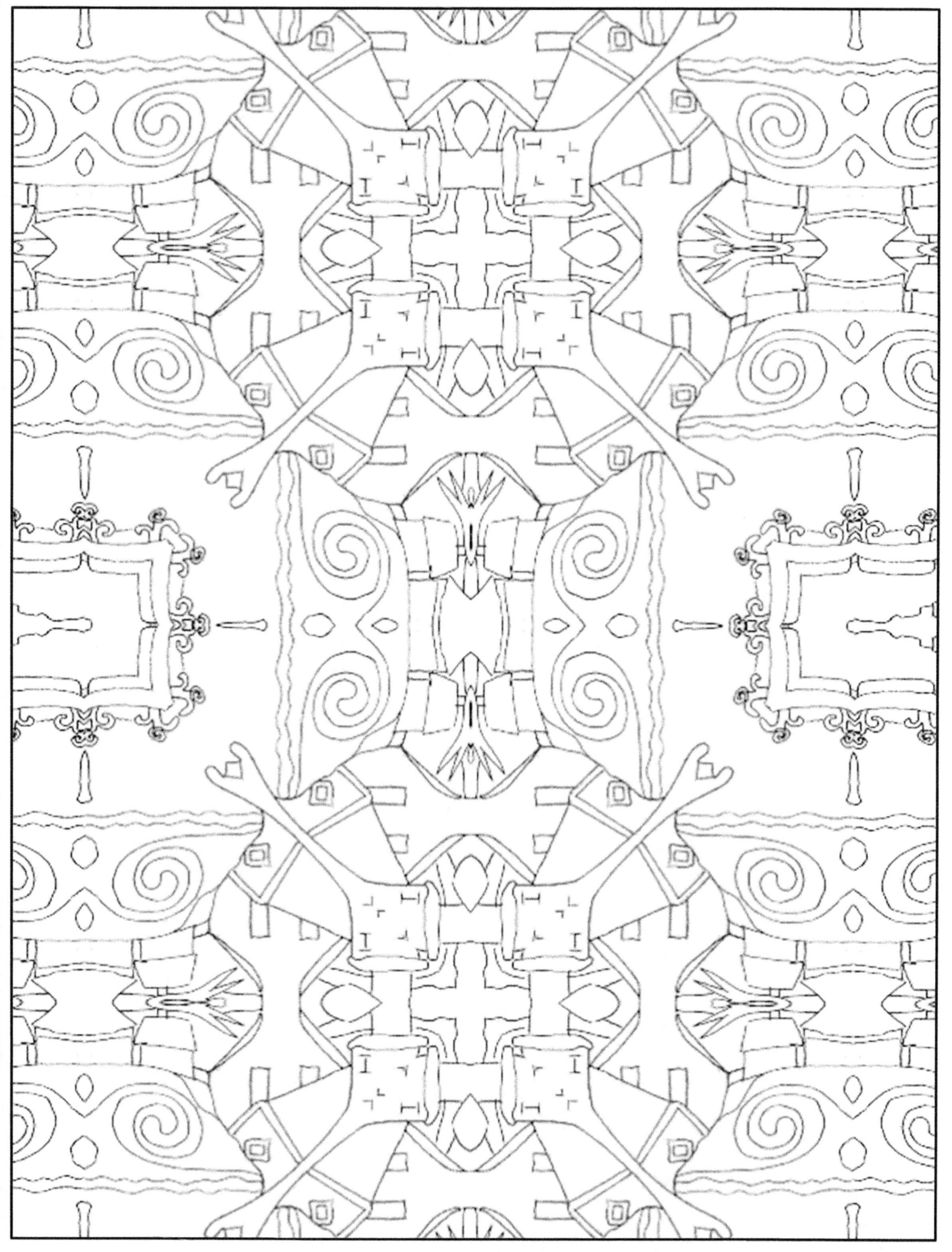

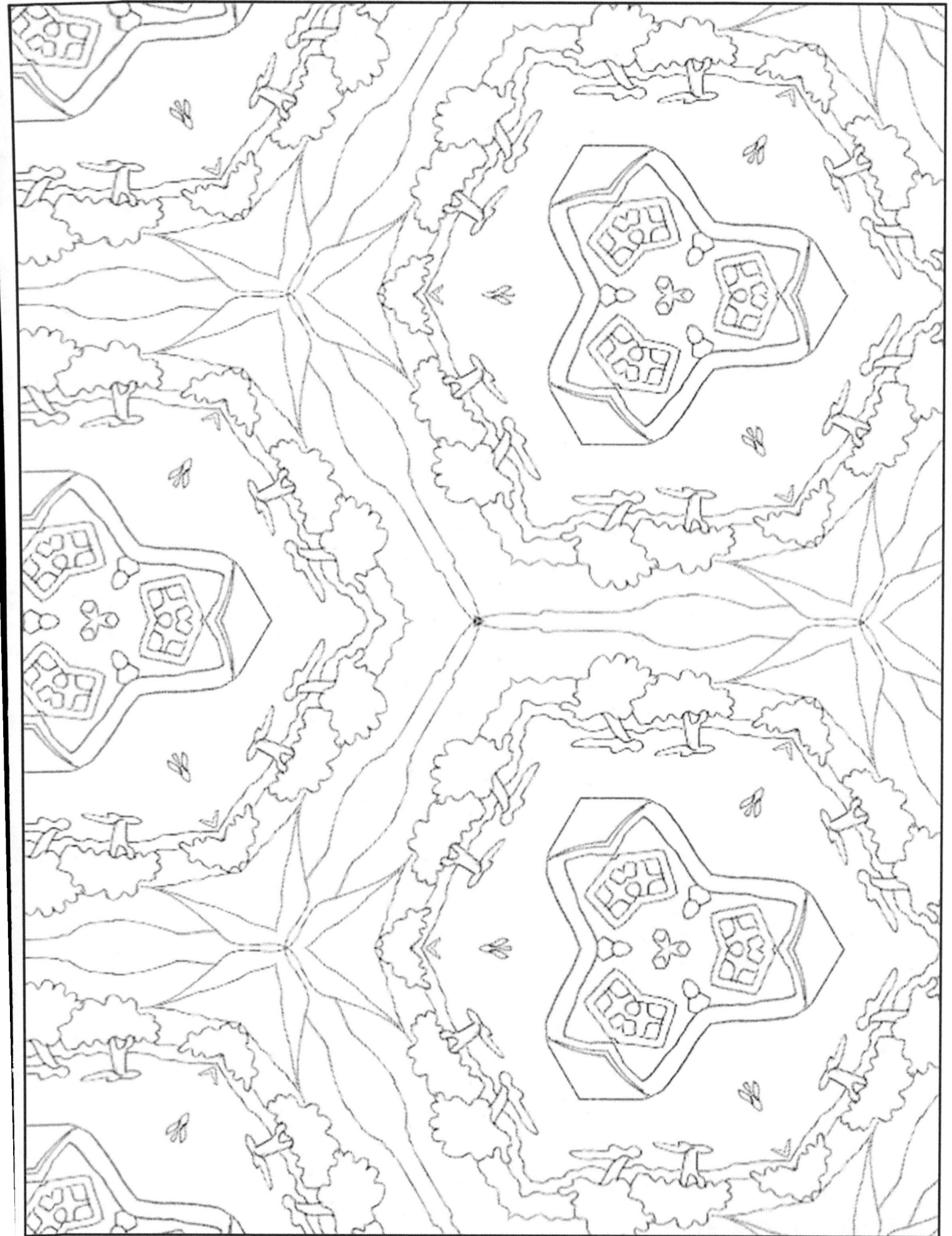

www.ingramcontent.com/pod-product-compliance
Lightning Source LLC
Chambersburg PA
CBHW080613190526
45169CB00007B/2990